Six Cherry Blossoms
and other stories

Also by Alicia Appleman-Jurman

Alicia: My Story

For information, visit www.aliciamystory.com

Six Cherry Blossoms and other stories

by

Alicia Appleman-Jurman

Desaware Publishing
San Jose, California

First Edition

ISBN: 978-1-936754-01-4
Library of Congress Control Number: 2012934488

Printed in the United States of America.

www.AliciaMyStory.com

Dedication

I dedicated my first book "Alicia: My Story" to the children who died in the Holocaust, in order to honor their memory.

This book is part of a legacy to my children and grandchildren – medor ledor – from generation to generation. My children are the second generation of a Holocaust survivor and my grandchildren are the third generation.

My dear sons Daniel and Zachary, daughter Roan and granddaughters Maya and Kendra – you are the recipients of this dedication and the legacy of our family's tragedy, as well as the tragedy and history of our people. Honor them by remembering.

This dedication is also in memory of Gabriel Appleman, beloved husband, father and grandfather. In his lifetime, he was a "Shomer Am Israel" – a guardian of the Jewish people.

May his memory be blessed.

I love you all very much.

Contents

Forward

For most of the world, Alicia is the girl immortalized in her book "Alicia: My Story" – the Holocaust survivor whose tale is inspirational, tragic and incredible.

For my sister, my brother, and I, she is, of course, just mom.

Frankly, we were quite lucky in that respect. You could hardly ask for a better mom.

The truth is, I didn't know about her story while I was growing up. She wasn't presenting her story regularly at that time – at least not anywhere I was present. I learned about the Holocaust in school with everyone else. It was only as a young adult that it suddenly clicked – all that stuff happened to *mom*.

Even after she wrote the book and began traveling and speaking extensively, Alicia *The Survivor* was always just one aspect of Alicia *The Mom* – and not the most important (to me at least). Part of this is, I think, to be expected – after all, my relationship with Alicia is over 50 years long, none of which overlapped the period covered in her memoir. But consider this: anyone who reads her book knows that Alicia is an extraordinary person. Is there any reason she would become less extraordinary afterwards? Indeed, those who know her well know that she did not become any less amazing once the war ended and she escaped Europe.

Part of our good fortune as her children is that we get to experience that first hand. But another part of that good fortune is that we get to hear the stories that didn't make it into the book. Stories that are just as interesting, and, to be perfectly honest, often more cheerful.

So it is my privilege, as her son (and now publisher), to share with you some other aspects of Alicia. I think you will agree with me that while she is always a survivor, she is often much more than that.

Daniel Appleman
San Jose, California 2012

Six Cherry Blossoms and other stories

Six Cherry Blossoms

In 1993, I was invited to tell the story "Alicia: My Story" to six graders at an elementary school in Elko, Nevada. Upon leaving the classroom, I was greeted by a student.

"Miss Alicia" he said, "our teacher told us about your book. I am now a third grader and will have to wait three years to hear your story. Could you please write a book for us?"

I was deeply moved by his request. I promised him I would try my best. We shook hands on my promise.

How do I tell such a tragic story to third, fourth, or fifth graders? Will they understand the cruel death of six million Jewish people, among them one and one half million children?

Yet I promised I would try.

For three months, I wrote in my mind. I became Blacky, and then Simon the blue jay. I felt their friendship and their commitment to each other's survival. I suddenly realized I was Blacky, and Simon represented the kind people who helped me during the Holocaust.

Thank you dear student for your inspiration.

Publisher's note:

This is a children's story. It is printed in a slightly larger font than the other stories, and without hyphenation, so children can read it on their own, or with their parents.

Six Cherry Blossoms

As I lay half-buried under the debris of the
devastated cherry orchard, I watched the
ashes dance like drunken sailors over the
fire-scorched ground where once stood a
grove of proud black-cherry trees. The
ashes were dancing, weeping, and lifting
the sparks into the air, swirling them round
and round, not wanting to let go of them.
As I watched, it seemed to me that they,
too, were as anguished as I was.

I am a little cherry branch, affectionately
called "Blacky", and this is my story.

Ours was an exceptionally large tree.
Four generations of branches bore juicy

cherries every year, and it was even said
that our old King, Gustav of Sedonia,
preferred our cherries above the others. I
was the youngest branch in our family and,
for some reason that even my mother
couldn't explain, I grew out of the top of her
branch instead of the side. This made me
the envy of my brothers and sisters but it
also had some disadvantages. I would shake
violently when the winds visited us.

But I also had a great view of the whole
orchard. I could clearly see the narrow, and
quite shallow, brook that ran around the
orchard, and then dropped into the
fishpond below. During the summer, the
clear cold water tinkled like musical bells
over the little stones and the cool grass.
Sometimes the sun reflected from the water
and I could see myself, as in a mirror. But
when the rains came, the little brook turned
into a roaring lion. At times I feared it that
it would flood the orchard and sweep me
along into the pond below. I even confided
my fears to my mother, but she comforted

me and assured me that I was safe, and that soon winter would come and the little brook would freeze solid.

Of all the seasons, spring was my favorite. My friends, the bees, came to pollinate the blossoms. I had only a few leaves on my body then, so they just nodded their heads in a friendly greeting, and flew into the branches among  the rest of my family. I felt sorry for myself, but only for a moment because I realized that I was very lucky to be part of such a magnificent cherry tree.

My favorite friend was a bird. He was a blue jay named Simon. He visited us when the cherries were already ripe. While eating cherries he told us the news from around our kingdom, Sedonia, and the neighboring country, Batavia. Although I didn't yet have any cherries for Simon to eat, he was very friendly to me. He probably thought I had a great future because of my exposure to the sun, and expected that eventually I would have many cherries for him.

But this year Simon came early, when all the cherries were still green. He greeted me briefly and flew directly to my great-grandfather's branch. I couldn't hear their conversation but I realized that something was wrong when I felt my mother tremble.

"Are you cold, mother dear, or are you perhaps sick?"

"Thank you, Blacky. I'm fine, don't worry." And, to reassure me, she stretched out her body, revealing beautiful clusters of green cherries.

"We will be all right until after the harvest", she then added, as though to herself.

"Mother, Simon flew in early and went directly to great-grandfather. I think something is happening..."

Before my mother could answer, the town bells began to ring, shattering the quiet of the morning. They rang for a long time and then a complete hush fell upon us. I felt my mother tremble again.

"Blacky", she said, "Simon did bring us news. Our old King Gustav is dead and his nephew Adrian will be our new king. You are too young to  remember him. Even as a child, he showed signs of cruelty. He used to break off a branch, and then, using both his hands, he would swing at our blossoms with all his strength. Later, as a young adult, I could see him looking at us as though he begrudged us the land we stood on. And now Simon has told us that Adrian plans to industrialize."

"Industrialize? What does that mean, mother?"

But my mother only lowered her head and remained silent.

As children sometimes do, I became interested in newer events and pushed the fears out of my mind. The harvest began. The villagers and their children came into the orchard, bringing with them lots of fun. They sang as they picked the cherries. They would eat some of them and exclaim, "How extraordinarily tasty is this year's harvest!" Our cherries were indeed very sweet and juicy.

In a way, I participated in the harvest. Once in a while I would get hit by one of my relatives when a picker would pull down a branch from above me and then let it go... or when a child looking for cherries would pull at me and then, disappointed, let go. I would sway back and forth pretending I was all grown up and important. But next year, I thought with anticipation, next year... just you wait, little guys! When my friend Simon flew back and apologized for ignoring me earlier, I nearly died from joy.

I was in this great state of mind when I heard the news Simon had just brought us. He repeated what he had overheard in the village.

"We must industrialize", declared our new King.

"Yes, indeed", agreed his ministers.

"To industrialize, we need more land and lumber", called the people of Sedonia.

"Land... and lumber?" echoed the trees in our orchard...

* * * * *

It was a beautiful sunny day in September when tragedy struck.

Men carrying saws and axes entered the orchard. Two men wearing red plaid shirts and carrying a big saw came to our tree. One of the men measured our trunk and wrote something in a small yellow pad.

"This one is a prince of a tree. Plenty of lumber here!"

"Ha! Ha! Ha!" laughed his partner, rubbing his big, calloused hands. "King Adrian will be pleased, I am sure. Ha! Ha! Ha!"

And then things began happening quickly. I heard the terrible sound of the saw. We began to shake.

"Timber!" came the call of doom, and we fell to the ground. I felt myself breaking away from my mother and flying. For a moment, I was suspended in the air, and then I fell into the little brook, half of me in the water and the other half resting on the soft soil of the bank.

I couldn't see the trees any more but I could hear the repeated calls of "Timber!" which were sentences of death for all of the trees in our orchard. As the day progressed, I could smell burning wood. I could see sparks going up in the air and taking with them pieces of my heart. Then the ashes and debris began drifting into the little brook.

I would have probably perished and disappeared in the bottom of our brook were it not for my friend, Simon the blue jay. There he stood; his feathers blackened and with an anguished look in his eyes. One look at him and my fears were confirmed. I started to cry.

"Yes, Blacky, we must leave Sedonia immediately", he said, and lifting me up in his beak, he carried me into the sky. I couldn't help but look down for the last time at the place of my birth. Nothing was left of my once-beautiful and proud orchard. The earth was being plowed under. I suddenly realized, with a deep pain inside me, that I was the only survivor of my whole family, and perhaps even of the whole orchard. It was then that I began to struggle with Simon. I wanted him to let go of me. I wanted to die with my family; to be plowed under. But Simon wouldn't hear of it.

"You must live, Blacky! You must. You are a witness to what happened here. You must live. One day King Adrian will pay for his crimes. When he is finished destroying his orchards he will probably invade Batavia and want to destroy theirs. They will fight him and will win the battle. They will make him pay for his destruction, you will see!"

So we flew on, and were near the Batavian border, when suddenly I heard a shot and Simon cried out in pain. Still holding on to me, he dropped into a thick bush. His head dropped against me, bounced slightly and lay still. I was sure that my dear friend was dead but then, to my great relief, I felt him breathing. Short, shallow, labored breaths, yet a sign of life.

"Please, Simon, live!" I cried as I prayed. "If it weren't for me you wouldn't have been wounded. I made you more visible to the cruel hunter. Please, Simon." Then, with a great effort, Simon moved his body close to me and fell into a deep sleep.

For five days, Simon fought for his life. The only drink he had was the dew that collected on my body. But he was a fighter and began to show signs of recovery. Then, suddenly, the weather turned very cold. Simon had to leave for a warmer climate. He tried to fly several times but I could see that he had trouble with his left wing, where the hunter's bullet struck him. He certainly wasn't strong enough to carry me.

"Simon, you must leave immediately. You must, if you want to live. You are strong enough, my friend; you can do it, but you

must leave me here. I will be all right and
when spring comes you can return and
carry me to Batavia and safety."

I pleaded with him for days, but he
wouldn't hear me. Finally, I realized that he
wouldn't leave without me and I agreed to
let him carry me just over the border into
Batavia and drop me as soon as we crossed.

I will never forget the effort Simon made
on this flight. He was leaning to the right
and breathing with difficulty. I really feared
for his life. But we were lucky; we crossed
the border safely and Simon found a very
nice home for me inside an apple tree. He
settled me into an abandoned birds nest.
He pushed until half of me was in the nest
and the other half anchored into the joint of
a cracked branch. Then he shook me to
make sure the winds wouldn't dislodge me,
touched me affectionately with his right
wing, and flew off into the sky. I watched
my brave friend struggle for a while. Then

he gained speed and disappeared over the horizon.

* * * * *

Soon winter came and the snow fell heavily upon the trees and on the earth. My nest was filled with beautiful snowflakes, each one a magnificent star. The branches of the apple tree bowed under the weight of the snow and looked very dignified. When the sun shone, a silver brilliancy enveloped us all, adding to the majesty of life. All this I could see but not feel. My heart was filled with sorrow and loneliness for my family and friends. I missed them terribly and I also worried about Simon. I hoped he had made it safely to a warm climate and that he would return to see me in the spring. Yet, I had a premonition I couldn't dispel.

I tried to occupy my mind by observing life around me. This orchard contained four other trees. We were near a farmer's white two-story home. I watched the constant movement of people between the house and a large red barn. I saw pails of milk, sacks of potatoes, braided ears of corn, garlic and onions carried from the barn to the house. Some days a colorful sleigh, filled with people, left the farm, drawn by horses whose bells tinkled as they passed the orchard.

One morning a lone rider stopped close to our tree. His horse's hoofs dug into the snow. A startled violet lifted her head, surprised to see snow all around her, and disappeared under the snow again when the rider moved on.

With the first signs of spring, I felt a change in my body. Without realizing what was happening, I had moved deeply into the crack in the apple branch and had become part of it. I grew stronger and all the fibers of my body and soul were nourished by the kindness of my benefactor.

I waited for Simon to return, but he didn't. Instead the farmer from the white house and his ten-year-old son came. The farmer carried pruning shears. He and his son stood under my tree. I watched in horror as the big pruning shears came closer and closer to me, almost touching me, when suddenly...

"Father, don't," called the boy, pulling his father's arm. "Can't you see the green leaves on the little branch? Please, father, don't cut the branch!"

For the first time since the tragedy of my orchard, I felt a glimmer of hope. There were kind people after all. I thought of my dear friend Simon and of the kind boy. I touched the branch, which had given me life, and I promised myself that I would make him proud of me.

I wasn't expecting to see the farmer and his son until harvest time and became very frightened when, one day, they stood under my tree again. The farmer held the pruning shears in his hand. I was going to be cut away after all. Couldn't he see...? But suddenly the boy called out excitedly and pointed his finger at me.

"Look, father, look at the little branch! Can you see it, father? Look, there are six cherry blossoms, and they are blooming on our apple tree!"

* * * * *

King Adrian attacked Batavia and was defeated. My poor country is now completely industrialized and not even one cherry tree is growing there.

I, dear children, survived. I still live on the apple tree in back of the white house. The young boy who saved my life twice is now an old man, but at harvest time he brings his family and friends to pick black juicy cherries from my branch. I never saw Simon again, but every so often, a blue jay would fly by, and seeing cherries on an apple tree, would look puzzled. I would always nod my head in welcome, but he would just fly on.

Perhaps you have guessed; my children and grandchildren grow apples on their branches. But very often a deep red streak will run through the white meat of their apples, and then one can taste the sweetness of a black cherry.

Childhood Memories

Readers of "Alicia: My Story" often ask what gave me the strength to survive. This story, I hope, will give you a good answer to this question.

It is not only about what gave me the strength, but also about the people in my life and how they contributed to my knowledge of how to survive.

My parents, brothers, grandparents, cousins, aunts and uncles educated me. They had faith in me and let me experience life in the mountains. My brothers taught me how to swim in swiftly moving rivers, and how to find food in the meadows and forest. I learned how not to be afraid when lost.

I must admit, I was a creative child, some may even say mischievous. I was disciplined with wisdom, but never with anger. My spirit was never broken. I loved and was loved by most of my large family. These memories gave me the strength to survive and even to reach out and help others during the Holocaust.

I regret not having been able to include "Childhood Memories" in "Alicia: My Story". This story and the chapter about my life in Cyprus would have increased the number of pages in the book to over 700 pages – too large for a book intended for children as young as sixth grade.

I am delighted to be able to make this story available to you now.

Childhood Memories

Of all the seasons, I think summer was the happiest time to be in Poland's Carpathian Mountains. The mountainsides grew bright green and were dotted all over with wild flowers; the sun bounced and danced off the river in ways it did not repeat throughout the rest of the year. Wild berries flourished in the woods, waiting for little children with straw baskets to come and pick them; fruits ripened in the orchards and the land sang with the voices of children home for summer vacation.

Summer was definitely my favorite time of the year, and my favorite year in the Carpathian Mountains was 1935, the year I was five years old. My name was Alicia, which is pronounced Aleet-zia in Polish. Since that time, I have been called by many names – Helka, Slavka, Ala, Alusia, Anusha, Ada, and now people know me as Alice; but it is when I was Alicia that I am writing about[1].

I was the only member of our family to have a Polish name. All my brothers had Hebrew names – Zachary, Baruch (Bunio), Moshe (Mosio), and Herzl. Only Herzl and I were not yet in school – he was a year younger than I was. The older boys went to school in our village, Rosulna, and studied with a Hebrew teacher in the afternoon.

As might be expected, growing up with four brothers had turned me into a regular tomboy. I climbed trees

---

[1] At the time this story was written, Alicia was indeed called Alice. However, since then she has returned to using her original name.

and played in the dirt. I swam fearlessly and ran around barefoot without thought of getting a thorn or splinter. And I was forever tagging after my older brothers, especially Zachary, my favorite.

When I look back, I can see it was those first few years growing up in the mountains that prepared me for what was to come later. Most Jewish children in Poland were city born and raised; they would never know how to live off the land as I did. It was unusual for Jewish families to have large land holdings in Poland, but then ours was an unusual family.

My mother's father, Grandfather Kurtz, was a well-to-do lumberman who immigrated to what was then the Austro-Hungarian Empire from Sweden. He had a good reason for coming. Eleven of his sixteen children were marriageable daughters, and Grandfather was looking for better Jewish husbands than he felt Sweden would be able to provide. He had visited America twice when my mother was a young girl; once he even brought her along with him. But his business interests, forestry and lumber, brought him to Minnesota. What did he find in Minnesota but more Swedes? So he left Sweden for the forested areas of the eastern wing of the Austro-Hungarian Empire, and settled his very large family in what had been Poland before an earlier war changed the borders. With the large Jewish population in this area, he had no trouble attracting suitable husbands for his girls.

We lived in an area known as Galicia, a far-eastern region now bordering on the Soviet Ukraine. Grandfather owned thousands of acres of land on either side of a river there, and for a long time employed a great many of the Hotsuli, the mountain people, as lumber-jacks.

I remember hurrying to the river with my brothers to wave to Grandfather and his crew as they drifted downstream on their rafts of freshly cut logs. There they would be, stripped to the waist, sunburned, gracefully wielding the long hooked poles used to break apart log jams. We could always pick out Grandfather by his long reddish beard, and if we could catch his attention, he would wave his hooked pole over his head to salute us. He was a rugged, powerful man, my grandfather, and had earned the affection as well as the respect of his lumberjacks.

My father, Sigmund Jurman, came to Galicia because of my mother. Father was actually born near Vienna in Austria. The son of a Rabbi, he was accepted into the military academy there at a time of severe prejudice against Jews. After graduation from the academy, he became an officer in the Austrian Cavalry. Papa was quick and brilliant and very charming, but it was very likely that his looks were just as important as his abilities in starting him out well in the world. He was tall and had a regal bearing, and his reddish-blond hair and clear blue-gray eyes were certainly an asset at a time when there were few Jews among the higher ranks of the army. Because he spoke Polish and Russian as fluently as his own German, he was sent to the Russian front when World War I broke out.

My father was not a man to shout out his accomplishments. But he was never without the gold medal given to him personally by the Austrian Emperor Franz Joseph, a high honor presented for bravery. Father always wore it on a chain around his neck. He received it for saving the lives of thirty Austrian officers who had been captured by the Russians.

Father's regiment knew that the men were being held under guard in a small synagogue in a nearby town. The original plan to save them involved a surprise attack and quick getaway on horses.

Unfortunately, or perhaps fortunately, depending on one's point of view, the planners realized that the Russians had horses just as swift as their own, and might easily have outrun and captured them. Then my father suggested a plan, which was accepted. He volunteered to go out on the mission alone. Dressed as a peasant, he tied a keg of vodka onto his saddle and rode into the Russian camp. He stank of the vodka. My father had splashed it over himself, gargled with it, and carried the alcohol into the camp singing and staggering. He loudly announced that he had come to honor the Russian victors.

The soldiers accepted father's story; at any rate, they certainly accepted his vodka. All night long, they passed the keg around the campfire, filling their tin cups again and again. Father drank enough to cast off suspicion, but since he had seemed drunk to begin with, the soldiers were pleased when he insisted they take most of the liquor themselves.

When the last drop had been drunk, and the last soldier lay snoring in a drunken stupor, Papa hurried to the synagogue, broke off the lock, and freed the prisoners. Then after "borrowing" the Russian's horses, they made their escape. As all little children do, I would ask to hear this wonderful tale over and over again.

It was the war that brought my father to Galicia, but it was my mother who caused him to stay.

My Grandmother Kurtz loved to tell the story of how my parents met. Grandmother Kurtz was a shrewd woman whose maternal instincts extended beyond her own large family to the entire Solotvina community. At that late stage of the war, many men from the area were missing. Some were off fighting, some dead, and their women and children often fell victim to the murdering Russian Cossacks who were part of the invading Russian army, and who had been known for generations as fierce Jew-killers.

When a handsome young Austrian cavalry officer appeared one day, with a detachment of soldiers, to commandeer a number of horses and wagons for the war effort, Grandmother gave them gladly, but she also persuaded the young officer, whose name was Jurman, to escort some of the local women and children several hundred miles west into Czechoslovakia. My father agreed and ended up leading 35 wagons into Prague! The people in the city must have thought it was an invasion.

Later, when asked why she had trusted the young man to return her horses and wagons, Grandmother Kurtz would smile and say, "The way he looked at Frieda, I knew he'd be back." And she was right; one look at my beautiful mother, then only sixteen, with her dark curly hair, creamy white complexion, and violet eyes, and my father was completely smitten.

But at war's end, when he returned to Galicia to court my mother, Father received an awful shock. Oh, the Kurtzes liked him will enough, very much in fact, but he was poor and they were rich. Mother was one of Grandfather's favorites. They wanted her to marry someone who would provide for her in the style to which she had been accustomed.

The situation could have ended tragically, with the young lovers never being allowed to marry, if my mother's older brother had not stepped in. Knowing it had long been Grandfather's dream to provide medical care for the poorer people in the community, my uncle flatly refused to continue medical school, unless his sister was allowed to marry Sigmund Jurman.

My grandparents raged, and Uncle's standing in the family was severely threatened. However, in the end, Mother was allowed to marry Father, and my uncle finished medical school.

My father never lost the feeling that he had not been considered suitable to marry my mother, and after leaving the army, he threw himself into a frenzy of moneymaking. A talented artist, he created designs in cloth for men's suits and coats, and sold them to fabric manufacturers. Twelve years and five children later, my parents were wealthy in their own right.

Papa would probably have preferred living in Vienna, far away from his in-laws, but he loved my mother, and my mother loved her family, so this most dutiful of sons-in-law built a house outside Rosulna on a piece of land owned by Grandfather Kurtz.

It was a big, wonderful house, built on top of a hill. Right next to the house was Father's warehouse, where he stored fabrics and completed garments for the upcoming fashion season. Father had dug a moat around the two buildings and diverted the river into it.

The moat was only three feet deep and no more than six feet wide, but after crossing the wooden bridge and mounting the steps to our front door, I felt it was like entering a fairytale castle.

Of our entire property, my favorite part was the orchard behind our house. It was not a large orchard, but we had several apple, pear, and black cherry trees. This particular summer I was making the most of them all. Each morning I was out of the house before eight and in the orchard breakfasting from our trees.

The main part of these "breakfasts" was the papierowki - "paper apples", as we called them in Polish. They were famous for their paper-thin skins and their sweetness. They were so juicy that they sprayed my face whenever I bit into them. I would look for these paper apples in the tall grasses that grew around and in the moat.

About the only thing associated with summer that I didn't like was Aunt Vitka and her seemingly endless visits. Aunt Vitka was the wife of another of my mother's brothers. She lived with her husband and children in Stanislavov, as did many of our relatives. Nearly every summer she would leave her husband at home and spend a month at our house in the mountains. Sometimes she brought her children along, as she had this summer, but just as often she came alone.

Aunt Vitka was a haughty bird, impressed with herself and her money. She liked to wear low-cut dresses and enjoyed free vacations with good-natured family members like us. But she made no secret of the fact that she did not approve of the way Frieda and Sigmund were bringing up their children. We were all but wild,

she felt; and I, being the only girl, was the worst offend-
er. Of course I had none of the poise or fine upbringing
that she gave her own children.

I would not go so far as to say I hated Aunt Vitka,
although I did find her an awful pest. Even at my young
age, I deeply resented Aunt Vitka and her constant
criticism. Mother was quite proper and highly refined,
and she taught us by example rather than by lecture.
She let us enjoy our childhood, but made certain we
were well mannered and schooled in the traditions of
our religion and our family. As a result, my brothers
and I had a keen sense of what was proper, and shared
an unspoken wish to make our parents proud.

My biggest problem with Aunt Vitka's visits was that
she loved the orchard almost as much as I did. Early in
her stay, she had moved one of our lawn chairs right
under my favorite apple tree, and every morning she
would sit and sun herself, staying at least an hour each
time. I usually solved this problem by getting out of the
house and into the apple tree long before she appeared.
But on one particular morning, I was running behind
schedule, having overslept.

When I realized how late it was, I threw on my
clothes and dashed out of the house. If I hurried,
maybe...

Aunt Vitka was nowhere in sight when I reached the
orchard, and rather than going first to the apple tree, as
I should have done, I decided to start breakfast by
climbing a black cherry tree instead. It was a beautiful
morning, and I rested on a limb with my back against
the tree trunk, munching on cherries and enjoying the
patterns of light the sun made as it filtered through the

leaves. Down in the grass I could see the robins and jays hunting for insects; the scene was so serene and heavenly, I quite lost track of time.

I had just picked my third handful of cherries when I heard the sound of approaching footsteps. Drat – there was Aunt Vitka. I peered through the leaves as she settled herself into the lawn chair. Oh, why hadn't I gone to that tree first? No telling how long she would be, and now not only could I not get to the apples, but if she spotted me coming out of the cherry tree I knew I would receive another lecture.

At least I was comfortably hidden, and had all the cherries I could want. Still, I did love those apples. There I sat, munching cherries and feeling sorry for myself, when I had a wicked idea. I decided that I would pelt Aunt Vitka with cherry pits. This, I hoped, would drive her from the orchard.

I was a skillful launcher of cherry pits, with experience gained through many "cherry pit wars" with my brothers. I chewed most of the fruit from the pit, positioned it between my thumb and forefinger, and sent it flying. The pit sailed out from under the leaves, through the lower branches of the apple tree, and splattered against Aunt Vitka's bosom, just above the low-cut of her dress bodice.

I giggled to myself as Aunt Vitka anxiously brushed away the sticky pit. A moment later, I launched my second volley, this time two half-eaten cherries at once. They flew through the leaves toward their target – this time one went off course a little and landed on her foot. She uttered a little shriek. This was wonderful!

I should have let well enough alone when Aunt Vitka did not leave after my first two attacks, but I was having such fun tormenting her this way. I could not resist a third assault. That was my undoing.

When the third pit hit her bosom and dropped down the front of her dress, Aunt Vitka sprang into action. "Frieda!" she called. "FreeDAAA!" with that high, shrill voice. Then I heard the screen door on the kitchen porch bang shut and realized, with a sense of impending doom, that my mother was on her way into the orchard.

What would happen to me as a result of all this was hard to predict. I knew I was wrong to pelt Aunt Vitka, but I had never expected to be found out either. Poor Mother was caught in the middle. She would have to punish me, and with Aunt Vitka breathing down her neck, she might be forced to do something extreme like spank me.

I clung desperately to the tree trunk, as the sound of my mother's footsteps grew nearer. "Did you call, Vitka?" she asked sweetly.

"Look here," Aunt Vitka said as she gathered up the sticky pits and displayed them huffily in her open hand. "Can you tell me why cherry pits would be falling from this apple tree?"

From my hiding place, I could see Mama's back as she bent over the out-stretched hand, studying the purple pits. She said nothing, but straightened and looked up into the apple tree. Aunt Vitka had not considered that it was naturally impossible for cherries to fall from an apple tree, but Mama most certainly had. She turned and stared directly at my cherry tree;

directly, I sensed with a child's fear of her parents' almighty powers, into my guilty eyes.

Then, in a move even more imposing, she took a step toward my tree and another, until she was close enough to hear me breathing. I clung to the branch and tried to hold my breath, fearful I might faint from excitement and come toppling out of the tree at my mother's feet.

Suddenly, my mother turned swiftly around and faced Aunt Vitka once more. "Most perplexing," she said, her voice taking on great tones of sympathy and consolation. "How fortunate your lovely dress wasn't stained, Vitka. Come; let's wipe away the sticky juice." And with that, my mother gently but firmly took my aunt by the elbow and steered her out of the orchard toward the house. I had been saved, but I knew it was only temporary.

* * * * *

I absolutely adored my father. I know that most little girls feel that their father is the handsomest, most wonderful father in the world, but I knew for a fact that mine was. He was so tall and strong, and he walked like a king, erect and poised. And handsome! Strawberry-blond hair, parted on the side and slicked back. A strong jaw, a regally carved nose. But it was the eyes that seemed the most impressive feature of Father's face. He had blue-grey, clear eyes that seemed to change color with moods. Papa's eyes could flash pale grey when he was angry, or dip into blue when he was happy. But more important, it was the expression in his eyes and the way he communicated with them that was

Father's gift. He had a way of looking people directly in their eyes when he talked with them. When he gave anyone his attention, that person felt as though he had suddenly become Father's only interest in life. A special lift of Papa's eyebrow could make people burst into laughter; the slightest frown filled one with sudden concern. And when something delighted or made him truly happy, I swear I could see those eyes twinkle.

My father worshiped my mother; courted her, and kept her in fresh flowers and pretty clothes. He would have given her anything she wanted. I like to think Mother was the dream Father had always had as a young boy, to marry a fairy princess and live happily ever after.

My aunts used to say, "the only time Sigmund's eyes turn dark blue is when he looks at his daughter." And they were right, in spirit. My father did adore me, and I worshiped him. He always told people that he had child after child until he finally got the daughter he wanted.

It was bliss being the child of such a princely man, and I did everything I could to please him. I had been polishing his riding boots since I was three and a half, and this year I had finally grown big enough so that I could reach my arm all the way down to the bottom of a boot without having to use a towel for extra length. Father was a great horse lover, ever since his cavalry days, and he wore riding breeches and boots nearly every day. Few men really look good in jodhpurs, but Father did. We had some beautiful horses, kept in a paddock outside the building at the bottom of the hill, which served as both garage and stable.

If I were asked whether Father had even a slight character flaw, I would have to say it was his stubborn pride. This was what prevented him from asking for help from my grandparents when we would soon be needing it – desperately.

I may have resembled my mother's side of the family physically, but spiritually I was my father's daughter. I shared his sense of fierce pride. I was strong willed, determined, and often indignant. This quality would both get me into great trouble and save my life on more than one occasion in the future.

But I did not know about the experiences that drove my Father to try to insulate his children from certain realities of life in Poland. He had grown up with the stings and slights of anti-Semitism, which still existed in supposedly enlightened Austria. He had seen his people slurred, treated shabbily, and frequently insulted by their countrymen. So Papa shielded and protected us as best he could. As a result, it wasn't for many years that I came to fully realize how cruel people could actually become.

* * * * *

September arrived. My three older brothers went back to school, leaving me terribly bored and restless. Herzl and I could only play together for a while before we tired of each other's company. We weren't allowed to bother Father while he was working, and Mother was too busy to entertain us all day; she often shooed us out from underfoot while she worked. I began wandering about our property, picking berries in the woods and watching the women from the village who came to our house to do the laundry.

On the day the laundresses came in September, I put on my new patent leather shoes and headed for the riverbank. Mother stopped me at the kitchen door and cautioned me not to get them muddy, or she would be very displeased. "You have play shoes for that, Alicia," she said. But I begged her to let me wear them, and I promised I would be very careful and not let anything happen to them. She reluctantly agreed, and off I went with the laundresses.

The laundresses would take laundry down to the water and, anchoring the baskets on the smooth stones, throw the sheets into the river so that the brisk current could rinse away the soapsuds. They would hold one corner so that sheets wouldn't get away from them, and then they would pull the sheets in, throw them back out, and pull them in again with a lovely rhythmic motion. Watching the sheets, which looked like sails, gave me a sudden inspiration. I quickly forgot my mother's warning.

I took off my shoes and stockings, and began hunting for small pebbles by the water. I collected handfuls of pebbles and filled my shoes to the brim. There they were – shoe boats! I decided to sail them down the current and follow along on the bank, taking them out later downstream. I thought it was a marvelous idea.

I carried the shoe boats to the water, set them afloat, and gave them a push. They bobbed up and down as they headed toward the center of the stream. All seemed to go well at first, but suddenly calamity struck

- they began to sink! I screamed as they disappeared from the surface.

All too late, I remembered Mother's admonition. I had only a single thought: get those shoes back! Without hesitation, I rushed into the water and began swimming toward my sunken shoes.

I was a good swimmer, at least for a child of five, but this was the first time I had ever been in this part of the river. Father always forbade it; he said the currents were too strong to take silly chances with something as precious as our lives. Even Zachary, who was quite tall and strong for his age, was ordered to stay away.

I tried to remain strong and resist the current, but I felt myself weakening. I was determined, however, to get those shoes and return to the shore. But the swift current overwhelmed me and soon I was swept downstream. Everything happened so quickly. The women heard my screams. As I struggled to keep my head above the water, I could see flashing images of women running along the shore, trying to keep up with me. I could hear shrieking, but the water was roaring in my ears so much that I couldn't really tell if the cries were coming from the laundresses or me.

The women quickly organized themselves. Wading hip-deep into the water, they began throwing white sheets toward me. I heard a voice crying, "Catch it! Catch the sheet!" But I passed quickly. They chased me along the shore again, this time spacing themselves farther apart and downstream from me. Again, I came upon the white sheets and began to grab and clutch, praying I would catch on to one. I brushed against something and caught hold. Next thing I knew I was being pulled to one side, against the current. Pulled, pulled, and finally strong arms reached around me and lifted me up. I clung blindly to my rescuer, my arms and legs locked around her body, my face buried in her neck. Holding me tightly to her, the woman waded to the shore. The others clustered around us. "Is she all right?" I could hear voices; "Is she breathing?" The woman carried me over to a rock and sat down, adjusting me on her lap. I was crying and coughing, and refused to let go of her. She held my head against her wet bosom and rocked me gently back and forth. Other hands reached down and stroked my back soothingly.

Suddenly I heard my mother's voice. "My baby!" she cried; "Where's my baby?" The circle of skirts surrounding me parted and Mother rushed through, wild-eyed and frantic. Seeing her caused me to burst into tears once more, and I held out my arms to her to pick me up.

Mother lifted me into her arms and my rescuer stood up, giving her the rock to sit on. Mother held me tightly and sobbed too.

"What happened?" Mother was frightened, and her fear made her aggressive, like a mother bear finding her cub in danger. "How did she get into the water?" The women looked at one another; none of them seemed to know.

"Ma'am, we didn't even notice her until it was too late," one of them ventured timidly. It was clear they were quite intimidated; no one had ever seen my mother so upset. Even I had never seen her like this.

"Alicia, please tell me what happened," she said. She spoke softly, but her voice lacked that soothing calm I had been hoping for. I looked up at her nervously. She gave me a gentle shake. "Tell me," she commanded.

There is a horrible queasy feeling that overcomes a child who knows she must admit a wrongdoing and face her punishment. I was feeling that way now. I turned my eyes away from Mother's face and stared at my knees. "I needed to get my shoes," I whispered.

She bent closer. "What?" she urged. "Speak up darling. You needed to get what?"

"My shoes," I repeated softly.

"Your shoes?" She straightened, looking very cross. "Alicia, what are you talking about?"

I swallowed hard and blurted out my confession. "My shoes sank in the water, Mama." I now spoke rapidly. "You told me not to get them muddy, and I didn't want you to be mad. So I had to get them back."

"What! You went into the river deliberately?" She spun me around so quickly I didn't realize what was happening until the first swats landed on my bottom. Briskly she spanked and spanked, and I cried out in pain and humiliation. All the women were standing around witnessing my punishment; I was so embarrassed. Finally, Mama pulled me back upright and gave me a little shake. "Wait until your Papa hears about this, young lady," she said fiercely. I trembled at the very thought. She set me on my feet and stood up holding tight to my hand.

"I'm so grateful to you all," she said to the women, her voice cracking with emotion. "I can't thank you enough. Mr. Jurman and I will always be in your debt for saving our little girl's life."

All of a sudden, she sounded so weak and vulnerable; I felt truly sorry for having given her such a scare. One of the women reached out and squeezed her shoulder assumingly, a gesture that under normal circumstances might have been considered out of place.

All the way back to the house Mother took such great hurried strides that I fairly flew along behind her, my feet hardly touching the ground. That night, when Father found out what had happened, I received another tremendous spanking, and for many months, I was absolutely forbidden to leave the yard without his or my mother's permission.

* * * * *

It's so ironic, really. All that water so close by in the moat and the river, and when we needed it the most, it did us no good at all.

It was November, and the days were cool, sometimes chilly. I don't really remember much about that particular Friday night. Mother and Father went to the synagogue after dinner, and Herzl and I went to bed at our regular time. The older boys were allowed to stay up a little longer.

After I was in bed and asleep, one of our servant girls climbed the stairs to the attic to get some apples. Nearly the entire attic was filled with crates of apples and pears, packed tightly in straw. Since the stairs were dark, the girl carried a candle with her. After she pulled out the apples she needed, she left the candle behind. With both hands managing the apples, the candle would illuminate the stairs for her trip back down.

But before she returned the candle tipped over, igniting the straw. By the time someone noticed the smoke, the roof was blazing. I have vague memories of being pulled out of bed and carried downstairs out of the house. The servant carrying me ran over the footbridge and set me down on the other side of the moat, along with Herzl and the other boys.

From a safe distance, we had a clear view of the horror that was to follow. Sparks from our roof were flying through the air as we watched the fire moving down through the house. Suddenly flames appeared on the roof of the warehouse next door. Only a few weeks before, Papa had finished stocking the warehouse; all of the merchandise for the spring season was there. Also there was the gasoline that we kept on top of the hill rather than down in the garage where it might be stolen.

It only took a few minutes for the fire to work its way through the roof and down into the warehouse, and then there was a tremendous explosion – the gasoline had ignited.

An hour later Mother and Father returned home unsuspecting, to find us all huddled in misery, trembling, our noses runny and our eyes red and teary. The last few flames were dying out and specks of ashes were still drifting down. Mother bunched us together and wrapped her coat around us. Father walked numbly around the smoking rubble of our home.

I will never forget the look on his face that night – the bewilderment, the disbelief, the shock that registered in his eyes. Everything he had worked for, and almost everything he owned in the world, had been wiped out in less than an hour.

And somehow, though adults would surely have dismissed it as a child's wild imaginings, I could not help but feel there was more to come.

Cyprus

This was originally intended to be the closing chapter of the book "Alicia: My Story". The book ends with the arrival of my ship, the Theodor Herzl, at the port of Haifa, just before it is about to be boarded by the British. This story continues from that point.

Cyprus

I recognized Hatikvah, the national anthem of Eretz Israel. I was moved to the depths of my soul and my eyes filled with tears as I hoarsely joined in singing its plaintive lyrics:

> "As long as the heart of the Jew beats
> And his eye is turned to the East,
> Our ancient hope still lives:
> To be a free people in Zion."

Together, hundreds of voices on the deck sang our national anthem; it was one of the noblest human experiences I have ever witnessed. And the British stood quietly by, allowing us to finish before they began disembarking procedures.

* * * * *

Somewhere a loudspeaker boomed. The commanding officer was requesting all the IJIs - Illegal Jewish Immigrants - to disembark quietly. The new name given us by the British didn't bother me at all. I was already a member of "Youth Aliyah" which meant that I was as close to the people living in Eretz Israel as I could be under the circumstances. The British could call me whatever name they chose; I knew who I was and was very proud of it.

British soldiers wearing red berets surrounded us to prevent our escape into the city as we took our first steps onto the Promised Land. I breathed the air in deeply and tiredly.

I turned for a last look at our valiant ship. It bore the name of Theodore Herzl, the father of Zionism. He was the great dreamer who said: "Im Tirtzu Ein zot Agada" which could be translated as "If you want something very much, it will not remain a dream!"

Yes, I thought bitterly, we had a dream, we have arrived in Eretz Israel. But some have paid with their lives. I could still hear the screams of the two youths who were thrown into the ocean by the British sailors who had boarded us. And I shuddered when I suddenly remembered how close I had come to being a victim myself.

Our ship looked sad and weary as we left it, but I thought rather proud to be a witness to the courage and fighting spirit of a desperate people. She knew that whatever her fate would be, she would live forever in the hearts of those she had carried for twenty-one days.

The British had set up a check post on the pier, which consisted of a table holding a registration book and some chairs. As each of us passed the table, one of the two soldiers at the table wrote down our names. We were searched, supposedly for weapons, but actually, it seemed to me, for valuables. A girl ahead of me in line refused to give up her fountain pen. She could not speak English and was screaming in Hebrew that the soldier had taken her fountain pen. I stepped forward and, in English, asked politely that he return her pen. He denied that he had taken it. I tried to explain to him that the girl was a student and that she needed her fountain pen.

"Where she is going she won't need a pen," he hissed cruelly.

I could see the pen sticking out of his shirt pocked so I reached out and tried to pull it away.

"You bloody Jewish bitch," he screamed, and grasped my wrist, holding it as in a vise.

"Let go of my wrist, you bloody child killer!" I was boiling mad and I am sure we would have come to blows if the other soldier, who until now had stood like a statue, hadn't give the girl back her fountain pen and shoved us both ahead. Because of this, my name was not entered in the book.

At the same time another fight was going on near us.

"Let me through to my children," I heard a middle-aged woman scream. I saw her holding two large baskets filled with fresh white bread rolls. She was part of the crowd of Haifa residents who had come to the Port to welcome us, but was kept from us by the police.

"You can't stop me, you bloody bastards!" By sheer body mass, she broke through the police line, and quickly distributed her rolls among us. I was lucky enough to get one, and as I was eating it, I could taste the salt from the tears of frustration that were now running down my face.

We were all loaded onto military prison ships and were soon on the way to Cyprus. Because we were not allowed on deck, I didn't see our actual departure, but I felt the sway of our ship as it turned away from Haifa. An unbearable pain spread inside me, reaching into the depth of my battered soul.

In a Concentration Camp on Cyprus

The Greeks call Cyprus "Love's Island" because Aphrodite, the Goddess of love, rose not as a child, but full grown out of the waves.

To me, Alicia Jurman, a prisoner of the British Navy, Cyprus was "The Eye of Hell".

It seemed to me then that the British were determined not only to kill us whenever possible, but to break our spirit as well. They hoped to achieve this by putting us into concentration camps.

The trucks carrying us wound their way through a fertile plain covered with fields of grain, olive trees, citrus groves and vineyards. The Island was very green and very beautiful. Only one thing marred its beauty, the concentration camp Caraolas near Famagusta.

I shall never forget the sight that met me as I got out of the truck. I saw a sea of tents on the sand surrounded by endless miles of ten-foot walls made of barbed wire. Tall watch towers, where the British posted sentries, were spaced along the walls.

Under the scorching sun, women in shorts stood in front of their tents, washing laundry in little pans. Men and women stood over open fires, cooking in tin pots and choking on the smoke. Near the barbed wire, half-naked children were looking longingly in the direction of the sea.

1947, I thought bitterly, and Jewish history is still being written in prison camps.

Our struggle with the British boarders and later forced transportation onto prison ships caused us to move very slowly.

Again, we were registered. We had to leave our money in the gate office. Regulations, the sergeant in charge said, but I thought it was plain robbery. I could see that very little money was collected. Few of us had any, and those who had, I hoped, were smart enough to hide it.

Our original group from Marquain, Belgium, stayed together and we were assigned to Youth Aliyah Camp number 65. The camp was separated from the other camps by a fence topped with barbed wire, and it had a small gate through which one entered. I recognized a young man from my hometown of Buczacz among the people who were standing on the other side of the fence, in camp 64. His name was Muniek. I had met him briefly in Salzburg, in Austria, after the war. I called out to him and he was very glad to see me. He had a bag filled with oranges and threw some over the fence to me. This was his way of telling me that he understood the shock I must be experiencing, and to remind me that the orange was our connection to the Land of Israel. His eyes also tried to express what his words could not: patience my friend, they were saying, this is the last stage before we will be able to be free, really free. Muniek's encouragement fell on deaf ears. All I felt was a terrible anger and an urge to escape from there.

While talking with Muniek, I felt myself beginning to itch all over my body. I looked at my arms and they were covered with a red rash. I told Muniek about it and he suggested that I see the camp nurse before I got settled. She turned out to be a very compassionate person. She suggested that I sleep in a separate tent until I could consult a Dr. Rappaport who was due to arrive from Eretz Israel the following day. In the meantime, she put a purple ointment on my body and gave me a small bottle to take with me to apply before I went to sleep.

Our group of sixty children collected blankets and towels from one corrugated metal hut, army cots from another, and were assigned tents. Some of the tents had two small rooms. I took one room and my friend Sarah shared the other with two girls called Esther. Forty-eight hours of total misery, I thought, as I put down my cot, spread the blanket, and lay down carefully. I tried not to touch my face, which for some unknown reason didn't have the rash. I pretended to sleep when Sarah called me to come and have supper. I needed to be alone. It was the 9th of May. I was seventeen years old.

Doctor Rappaport decided that my rash was an emotional protest against my imprisonment in the concentration camp, and all he said he could do for me was ease the itching with ointments. In a way, it was good news, but I suffered greatly from constant scratching, and from the blue or purple ointments, which made me look like a clown when I forgot and touched my face.

My rash was further irritated by my clothing, which was not at all suitable for the very hot weather we were having on the Island. One afternoon, as I was resting on my cot, I noticed a tear in the side of my tent. The tent wall was made of three layers of cloth. I saw an inside layer of blue material and realized that it could be a solution to my problem. I used my scissors, made a careful incision in the tent wall and removed a piece of the inner blue layer. The fabric was a little stiff, but of good quality, and seemed to be cotton, which would wash well. This discovery soon turned out to be the best thing that happened to me since I arrived. I shared it with all my friends, and we were soon busy sewing short sleeved or sleeveless blouses and shorts. Suddenly, our part of the camp blossomed in all blue outfits. I don't know whether the British ever noticed what was happening to their tents. I hoped not, because we were very careful to close the outer linings of the tents after we cut out the inside.

A week after we were settled into our tents we were moved again, this time into large corrugated metal buildings with arching roofs. Each of the buildings held twenty steel beds with straw mattresses. Ordinarily I would have considered this an improvement over the tents, but it was summer and the heat that was beating down on the roofs of the buildings radiated inside, making them unbearably hot and stuffy.

Because of the heat, we rose at five in the morning and stood in line to get water in Camp 64, where one of the barracks housed water faucets. We had running water one hour daily for all four camps, which housed close to four thousand people. At six o'clock, we had breakfast and at seven, we started classes. Our class of twenty boys and girls aged sixteen to seventeen was considered the senior class. We had two young teachers from Eretz Israel, Moshe and Yaakov. They were both volunteers from Kibbutzim, communal farms, and we loved them. We also had a young man from Hungary, a survivor like ourselves, who taught us Jewish History and Hebrew composition. His name was also Moshe so we called him Moshe-Moshe. He always would answer us "I hear you — I hear you".

We stopped our lessons at one o'clock, had our lunch, washed our laundry, did our homework and resumed classes from four until six. Since we didn't have any lights, we were forced to go to sleep early. Those who wished to sit outside and read improvised a lamp from a tin containing a wick and kerosene. I was one of those who did so; it was a smoky adventure.

I wouldn't want to give the impression that I adjusted well to my new life - not at all. I was very unhappy, especially when I looked at the barbed wire that surrounded us. Many times, I thought of escaping from the camp, and even shared those thoughts with my friends Sarah and Muniek. Sarah and I visited Muniek occasionally and he was always very kind to us. He still had a supply of oranges that he gladly shared with us. He kept them hidden inside his boots. At times when he wasn't in his barracks, we just went up to the boots that stood near his bed and helped ourselves.

Muniek listened very thoughtfully when I confided in him about my need to escape from the camp. It wasn't only that my rash was driving me mad, but my spirit, which had rallied under terrible conditions in the past, was now trapped in a cage of barbed wire and was turning and tossing within me, causing me great anguish.

"I have to be free; I have to get out of here now!" I cried with passion, facing Muniek. But he would always advise me to wait and see what would happen. He said that even though we didn't see or hear anything in that miserable camp, things were happening around us and soon we would become aware of changes.

Muniek's predictions were correct, because soon after our discussion, our camp started a training program under the guidance of members of the Palmach. The Palmach, the special striking force of the Jewish Defense Organization called the Haganah, was established in 1941 when Rommel was at the gates of Palestine. The British, grateful for their help, had trained hundreds of young Jewish men and women as guerrilla fighters. In Europe during the war, valiant Palmach men and women parachuted behind the Nazi lines to bring word to trapped Jews that they were not forgotten, and to fight with the partisans. Now, in the middle of the "White Paper War" waged by the British against the survivors of Hitler's terror, the Palmach came to support and train us in self-defense. The training was with heavy wooden sticks and was called the "Shmor rosh" -"Guard your head" tactic.

Since we could only train at night, it was unavoidable that some of us would receive head injuries, yet we applied ourselves to learning the art of self-defense. We also had lectures on tactics and world politics. One exercise that we absolutely hated involved crawling under the barbed wire that separated our camps. We tore our clothing and the skin on our bodies. All this aggravated my rash so that, when I was not bleeding from barbed wire scratches, I was bleeding from scratching my rash. However, all this activity, and the quality and dedication of our trainers, did to some extent protect my spirit from breaking.

Our trainers, who we called "Palmachniks", trained us in self-defense during the night, and taught us a variety of other subjects during the day in classes conducted in camp 64. One of them was Yoram, a tall blond blue eyed "Sabra" (native-born son of Eretz Israel). He was a doctor, an intern at a hospital in Jerusalem, and he had volunteered to come to Cyprus for the summer to teach. Five students from our group asked Moshe's permission to attend Yoram' s classes, but four dropped out and I was the only one who remained. Yoram had about thirty students drawn from all the camps, of all ages. It was a wonderful class, and since I was already familiar with most of the material he was teaching in biology, I concentrated on Chemistry, which, I must admit, wasn't my favorite subject. I studied very hard though, and was able to keep up with the class, because Yoram always encouraged me.

I liked Yoram from the moment when, during the "Guard your head" exercises, he handed me a wooden stick and told me that, since I was tall and could reach out over the top of the head before me, I should be able to master that art easily and safely. He was taller than I was, and when he exercised with me, I learned quickly.

He paid special attention to my training and even gave me a supply of ointment to put on my wounds. His concern as a physician always came first.

We seemed to be running into each other often. One time I was sitting under one of the dry bushes and crying. My crying spell was due to a combination of several things. A few days earlier, the winds had swept through our camp and carried off the laundry that we hung up to dry on the bushes. The rain that followed soaked it and now our laundry lay all clumped up like little animals heaving their last breath. The short storm left my eyes and mouth filled with sand. The final incident that triggered my crying had occurred in our classroom. Moshe-Moshe had asked us to write an essay. Usually, knowing myself to be a poor speller, I would rewrite everything before handing it in. But I didn't this time. The essay was judged to be well written and very interesting, and it was chosen to be published in a newsletter that was being organized in our Youth Camp.

Instead of returning the paper to me for correction, Moshe-Moshe gave it to one of the Esthers to rewrite. She complained bitterly about that assignment and said she thought that my essay shouldn't have been selected for the honor. I happened to overhear her say so and instead of just ignoring the matter and taking the essay from her, I ran to the far end of our camp, sat under the dry bush, and cried.

Suddenly, a white handkerchief appeared in front of me. When I looked up, I saw Yoram smiling at me. I buried my face in the handkerchief and sobbed as though my heart was going to break. He stood there not saying a word. Like a wound up clock, my emotions eventually ran themselves down and I was able to thank Yoram.

I returned the handkerchief to Yoram in our biology class the same afternoon. Our subject was the heart and how it functioned. He pinned drawings of the heart on the wall and distributed smaller copies to each student.

As on other occasions, Yoram used humor whenever possible. The heart, he said, is the romantic organ in our body. It is used to express emotions, for example: "I love you with all my heart". As he said this, he looked straight at me. Our eyes locked for a moment and I felt an electric shock running through my body. I felt myself blushing deeply. I sensed rather than saw some heads turn in my direction, and at that moment, I wished I could just disappear.

Yoram only meant this as part of his discussion, I told myself. He was twenty-five or twenty-six and couldn't possibly be interested in a seventeen-year-old girl. Still, we did keep running into each other. Had he stayed in our camp longer, I might have fallen in love with him. He reminded me of my childhood friend Milek, especially his captivating smile. Although I had met several boys I liked, Yoram was the first person who touched my heart; really touched my heart. But I kept my feelings to myself because I knew he was returning to Jerusalem to his own life, and that a long time would pass before I would see him.

I never saw Yoram again. He was killed during the War of Independence in 1948, near the gate of the old city of Jerusalem. He was there to help remove Jewish children before the Jewish Quarter was lost to the Jordanian Arab Legion. I grieved for him for a long time.

One of the reasons the British couldn't really break our spirits was because our life in camp was like a small smoldering volcano that erupted from time to time. From our Israeli teachers we learned what was happening in Eretz Israel. The Haganah had gone underground; many of its leaders had been arrested and put into prison. The Etzel movement, the Far right, was active against the British, with hangings, and retaliatory hangings, by both parties. The gates of Palestine remained blocked by the British Navy.

Our camp, in solidarity with the people of Eretz Israel and the survivors in Europe, declared a hunger strike. I remember the days well, not only because we were hungry, but also because I had a rather heated conversation with a Scottish Major who was part of the regiment in charge of the camps. I had noticed him at the gate when we arrived, not only because he was wearing a kilt, which was very similar in design to the skirt I was given before I left Belgium, but because there was compassion in his eyes when he looked at me. I was very confused by him, because I wanted to hate my captors and I couldn't hate him. I saw him several times when he stood talking with Israelis. Once I literally ran into him and again was very confused to see sympathy in his eyes.

He entered our barracks on the second day of our hunger strike. We were all lying on our beds, resting, sleeping, or reading and trying not to think about the churning inside our stomachs. The major called out a greeting and asked if anyone spoke English. When I said I did he came up to my bed and, after asking permission to sit down near me, began talking.

"What I can't understand is why your teachers allow you, children, to fast in this heat. Perhaps you can enlighten me?" he asked with a hidden passion in his voice.

"Major, Sir," I spoke slowly trying to pronounce each word clearly, and searching for the right words. "The children you refer to stopped being children at the age of ten or younger, when Hitler and his butchers destroyed their families. So don't worry about that. And the reason we are striking is because even now, after the war, we are still being held in concentration camps. Instead of helping our people in Palestine and rewarding them for fighting Hitler you are imprisoning and hanging them, just to please the Arabs and their Mufti who were known friends of Hitler. Is this the way to act? I ask you as a Scotsman."

My voice was beginning to crack so I stopped talking. The major stood up, but before he left, I had a glimpse of his face and what I saw really shocked me. Could it be that I had met one human being, who really cared what happened to me - to us? Was this Scottish Major that rare human being, I asked myself, as I turned to face the wall.

Toward the end of August, we were notified by the authorities that anyone who wished to go swimming in the ocean should assemble at the front gate of the camp. About two hundred of us set out on a walk to the ocean. I can imagine that from the air, we must have looked like a large caterpillar as we moved on the road surrounded by jeeps and half-tracks filled with armed soldiers. Seeing our group surrounded by soldiers with guns brought back some terrible memories, but the reason I opted to go for the swim was my love for the water and because I hoped to be able to feel some measure of freedom. I was wrong. We could, however, make a choice. We chose to sing Hebrew songs all the way to the sea.

The beach was completely deserted and the water was placid, with gentle waves climbing up the sand. I

dropped my towel, took off my sandals and, still wearing my shorts and blouse (we didn't have bathing suits),
dived into the first wave. It felt cool and wonderful. I let
myself rock back and forth on the incoming waves and
then swam out into quiet waters close to four floating
barrels. I let my imagination run away, decided that
where I was, was Cyprus, and beyond the barrels was
the ocean that led to Eretz Israel and freedom. I dived
under the barrels and started swimming vigorously out
into the ocean. I looked back and could see that the
people were getting smaller. Just as I decided to turn
back, I heard shots followed by a loudspeaker calling to
me to turn back. Then there were more shots. For a
moment, I thought that my friends were being massa-
cred on the beach and I began to panic. Then the
loudspeaker, calling me a "Bloody Jewish bitch", told
me if I didn't return immediately they would shoot at
me instead of in the air. I started back but took my
time, because I was trying to control the anger in me
caused by their name-calling. When I got to the edge of
the water, I was picked up by two very angry soldiers
and thrown back onto the water. I fell badly and hurt
my ankle.

Now it was my turn to call them bloody so and so's
and if it were not for the Scottish Major who had
accompanied us, I would have had to fight those two big
bullies.

He now stood between the soldiers and me and tried
to help me get up. Extending his hand, he pulled me
slowly to my feet. I winced as I tried to stand on my
uninjured leg. Using both of his hands, he supported
me and, for a fleeting moment, I thought that he was

going to take me in his arms but instead he said, "You will have to ride in the jeep, lass, you can't walk all the way back. Lean on me, gently now," and he tried to guide me to his jeep. But I only stood there. It would have been unthinkable for me to ride in a British jeep; even with what I was now convinced was a most compassionate human being. So I thanked him with my eyes, tied my towel around my ankle and, feeling the pain with each step, I limped stubbornly all the way back to camp. I am sorry to say that I slowed our procession considerably, but at that time it was worth it to me. No one sang as we returned, perhaps because we were tired, or perhaps everyone was angry at the way the soldiers had treated me. I could see some of the soldiers still eyeing me angrily. I was sure they didn't like our slow pace in returning, or the language I had used to them. Well, I thought, I learned the language I had used from them; they used the word bloody all the time when referring to us. I hated the word, but if words were the only weapon I could use to fight my captors, use them I would.

Winter arrived and suddenly a kind of excitement swept through all the camps with rumors flying back and forth about important events about to take place.

I will always remember November 29th, 1947 as a very special day in my life. At Lake Success in New York, the nations of the world were about to vote on the recommendations of the United Nations Special Committee for Palestine as to whether or not Palestine should be partitioned into a Jewish State and an Arab State.

It was a day mixed with agony and excitement, and finally we heard that thirty-three nations had voted in favor, thirteen were opposed, and eleven had abstained. THE JEWISH STATE WAS BORN.

It was a very emotional day in our lives. We sang Hebrew songs and hugged each other. We wouldn't have been surprised if Moses had suddenly appeared and, parting the sea, had led us to the Promised Land; such was our state of mine. In the meantime, new rumors flew about our camp. An important official of the Jewish Agency was negotiating the release of all the Youth Aliyah children from Cyprus. The rumor became reality and within a few days, I was actually standing in front of the main gate through which we had entered at the beginning of the year. We had our bundles ready, and in small groups we were soon led through the gate, registered in the office and then loaded onto trucks.

Just before I was to get into the truck the Scottish Major came up to me. He extended his hand and I gave him mine. "If there are more like you in Palestine, Lass, then the country has nothing to worry about. But you really have to watch your temper." I blushed and just looked at him, and it took all my will power not to walk into his arms.

As our trucks pulled away, I saw people standing near the barbed wire waving to us. "Shalom" we all called out; see you soon in Eretz Israel". And as the trucks turned away from the camp, I saw the major standing there. He seemed so alone. Is it possible that I would miss him? Part of me thought myself a stupid idiot. How could I miss a Scottish Englishman? And part of me said yes, and rejoiced because I had found goodness, a real good human being.

My return trip to Haifa was on a Greek ship. My friend Sarah and I shared a cabin. It was a lovely cabin with white sheets on the bunks and excellent food that, because I was excited, I could not eat. Since I was known to be a good sailor, Sarah suggested that I take the upper bunk, but we were in for a surprise. I was very seasick all night. I threw up all over Sarah when she tried to help me down from my bunk. Sarah was hysterical with laughter. Luxury didn't agree with me at all, she said. I was only a good sailor on a leaky boat. She promised not to tell anybody so that I could retain my reputation. But a miracle did happen on that boat. The itchy rash, which had made my life miserable during my entire stay in Cyprus, had completely disappeared. Only the bleeding wounds where I had scratched myself remained.

I was up early and stood on the deck holding my knapsack ready. The sun had not yet come out and I could see the twinkling lights coming from the Haifa-Carmel hills. They looked joyous, matching the joy in my own heart. They seemed to be calling to me:

"Baruch Haba, Alicia"
"Welcome home, Alicia"

Photographs

I met the captain of the Theodor Herzl again in 1949, and he gave me some pictures of the ship. I was then serving in the new Israeli Navy and he had become its commander.

The Theodor Herzl displayed the Star of David and two banners: "The Germans destroyed our families and homes; don't you destroy our hopes," and "You joined the navy to chase orphans."

The ship was leaking and all those who were able were bailing. The Theodor Herzl was trying to pass as an ordinary freighter, so all but the crew had to remain below without fresh air until nightfall. Most of us suffered from seasickness.

Sixteen miles from Haifa, we were stopped by British destroyers. Our captain pleaded through a bullhorn, "The people on board are survivors... many are sick. Many are orphans... let us come home." Their answer was to ram the ship repeatedly for two hours.

For two hours, we threw cans filled with garbage onto their decks, but when they decided to board, we stood no chance. First came tear gas, still, we fought a pitched battle.

Six children died from being hit by rifle butts. Others were thrown overboard and drowned, or crushed between the ships. I only escaped that fate by giving a black eye to the soldier who tried to throw me in to the ocean.

This photo shows the coffins of the dead children being carried off the ship by the British.

In Cyprus, we were assigned tents. There was no shade and I was very hot in my wool kilt, but I soon noticed that the tents had a lining of blue fabric that I used to make shirts and shorts for myself and for the others. Shortly after that, we were put into corrugated metal huts.

I Love Israel

I am a perennial student. I love going to school. At the age of fifty-seven, I was still a student at Fullerton College in Fullerton, California.

I was taking a class in creative writing taught by Professor James Blaylock. I wrote most of my stories about my experience during the Holocaust. We read the stories in class and the students commented on them.

After I finished reading "A Cry in the Night" one of the students asked me "Alicia, why do you always write sad stories?" He was a very nice young man and I felt guilty subjecting him to sadness.

"You are right," I apologized. "Next time I will write a happy story."

This is how "I Love Israel" was written. He liked the story.

However, I promised on my brother Zachary's grave and I promised my mother that I would bear witness to what happened to us. I continued writing sad stories.

I Love Israel

It was December 1947, my first day in my new school in Israel - Mikveh Israel - "The Hope of Israel".

After arriving in Israel, I was given a choice of schools to attend. I chose Mikveh Israel for two reasons. It had a strong science curriculum, and the name itself, "The Hope of Israel", was very appealing to me. I had lived through the genocide of my people by Nazi Germany, and, after my recent release from a British concentration camp in Cyprus, I needed to hope for a good future. What better place could I have chosen?

In 1947, Mikveh Israel was, and still remains, one of the best agricultural schools in Israel. Founded over one hundred years ago by the French-Jewish Alliance organization, it educated the pioneers of the 1800's and early 1900's who came to build what was then known as Palestine. Later their sons, the "Sabras", attended this predominantly boy's school as well. Only after World War II did the school become co-educational, when children, survivors of the Holocaust, were sent to Mikveh Israel by the Youth Aliyah organization, sponsored by Hadassah.

Mikveh Israel is located in the center of Israel. Its borders are a large city, Tel-Aviv, and a smaller city, Cholon. It includes hundreds of acres of fertile land and well-tended fruit orchards. At the time, close to three hundred students and faculty lived in dormitories and a few small houses. The land was cultivated under the supervision of teachers who taught the students for six hours in classrooms and three hours in the fields. Most of the food was grown for local consumption, with the exception of numerous varieties of flowers, citrus fruits and tomatoes. Those were sold in Tel-Aviv and used to buy clothing, books, and other things the students might need.

On Saturdays, one could see the city people strolling with their families through the colorful and aromatic botanical gardens, sitting under the orange and grape-fruit trees, eating their lunches or reading and sometimes sleeping on blankets under the trees.

An elderly guard stood at the gate of the school grounds when I arrived there on December 20, 1947. I handed him my referral paper from Youth Aliyah. He looked at it, and then nodded his head. I was just about to walk through the open gate when he stopped me.

"Wait a moment please." He took an orange from a crate next to him.

"Look, the first thing you learn here is how to peel an orange." Using his fingers cleverly, he stripped the fruit and handed the peeled orange to me. Holding it tender-ly in my hand, I brought it to my nose, inhaled the sharp and refreshing aroma, put it to my lips, and kissed it. Then I turned away from the guard and swiftly walked through the gate, trying desperately to fight the tears that threatened to spill all over my face.

The dirt road leading to the school buildings was lined on both sides with tall and very graceful palm trees. They appeared to me like guards of honor or angels of peace on the road to paradise. The sun played along the road, casting tall shadows that only enhanced that beautiful December day.

The smell of freshly plowed earth was all around me and once in a while, when the wind picked up, I could smell roses from some hidden garden. It seemed to me that nature itself was welcoming me to my new home. It seemed to call out to my soul. Suddenly, I felt such joy inside me that I thought I would burst into a thousand pieces.

The road suddenly turned right, revealing a most interesting sight – and colorful head-kerchiefs and khaki sun hats popping up and down between long rows of tall green plants. As I neared the field, I saw teenage boys and girls, apparently students from the school. They were busy lifting tomato plants onto rounded, sturdy wooden poles where they would tie them together with thin ropes. I was fascinated by the rhythm of their movements. They pruned the leaves of the plants and gently lifted the still green tomatoes over the ropes, letting them rest against the poles facing the sun. The boys and girls sang as they worked but were occasionally interrupted by instructions from an older man, apparently their teacher. He sent several of them back to correct some of their work, talking to them as they worked, and waiting for them to finish and rejoin the front rows.

I was so engrossed watching the tomato field that I didn't hear the horse and wagon approach until they were almost upon me.

"Hey! Are you crazy! Get out of the way!"

I turned to see two boys sitting on the wagon bench, one of whom was pulling on the reins of a chestnut horse. I moved backward quickly, tripped over a tree stump and fell on my back. The orange rolled out of my hand onto the dirt road, my knapsack slid off my shoulder and fell into the ditch, and I lay stunned with my head in the ditch, and my long legs anchored in the tree stump. My pleated skirt rode up over my stomach, exposing my underwear. For moment, I didn't know whether to cry or laugh. I must have done a little of both while trying to pull the skirt over my legs, a motion which only moved me deeper into the ditch with my legs flying in the air.

But nothing, nothing in this world could have spoiled that beautiful day for me. The two tall and very handsome boys finally helped me to my feet. I blushed with embarrassment thinking about my fall, but I soon recovered. The boys politely offered me a ride in their hay wagon and I accepted, but I noticed a meaningful look pass between them when, after I was seated on the bench, they suggested that I try driving the wagon to the barn.

Oh, I thought, they want to have some fun; a new student - why not? I took the reins in my hands, wound them double over my fingers and let the horse trot gently. Then I let out a loud cry and, hitting the back of the horse with the reins, we took off.

The two boys tumbled into the hay and screamed for me to stop. But I drove for about ten minutes at full speed until I reached the barn. Fool a farm girl, would they? What a splendid day that was!

This is my student identification card from Mikveh Israel

Here I am picking oranges at Mikveh Israel. This could be dangerous work because the Arabs, who possessed British weapons, often fired upon us in the fields. On this particular day, that is exactly what happened, but the bullet (Which I still have) hit a branch in front of my chest and fell to my feet. My friend had a camera and wanted me to climb back up and pose for a picture, and foolish girl that I was, I did it!

Acknowledgements

Two weeks ago, my son Daniel came to Shabbat dinner and handed me a folder. I opened it and found a printed and illustrated page titled "Six Cherry Blossoms" and Other Stories.

My heart skipped and I felt a powerful emotion going through me. I was looking at the printout of my second book.

After twenty-four years, I present these stories to my beloved readers.

I don't have the words to thank my son for the years of dedication and hard work and love he has shown me during the years I bore witness to the tragedy of the Holocaust. His dedication to get the book published through Desaware Publishing is outstanding and very moving. It takes great courage to get involved with a survivor, especially when the survivor is his mother. Inviting me to tell my story to his youth group, reading the moving and beautiful letters from students, teachers and those who read "Alicia: My Story" – Daniel dear, thank you and I love you dearly.

"Six Cherry Blossoms" has lovely illustrations of Blacky the cherry branch and Simon the blue jay by my daughter Roan. She also inspired me and listened to my story since she was ten years old. One time, when we celebrated Passover, she asked me "Mommy, don't you have a mommy, daddy, brother or sisters?" What could I say to a six-year-old daughter? I told her they died in the war.

As a survivor, I carry the pain inside me of the loss of all my family. I realized it would be wrong to try to lighten my pain (if this were possible) by sharing it with my children. If I were to tell them what happened during the Holocaust, I would have to include events after the Holocaust, when I came to Eretz Israel, then called Palestine. They would need to know how brave Jewish children can be when they have a chance to face the enemy and are able to defend themselves. I would share with them pride in the rebirth of Israel and, most of all, the heritage of honor of those who died during the Holocaust, their family, and our people. Roan understood all this and was very generous with her love and respect.

My son, Zachary, was always respectful, and loving, and gifted his friends with "Alicia: My Story".

My darling granddaughters Maya and Kendra invited me to their school to tell my story. They introduced me with pride and love. They are our future, and, as third generation of a survivor, they will contribute to the welfare of the Jewish people and American Jews.

I would like to give my love and thank the many teachers who teach the Holocaust in their classrooms, and the students who asked me to write "Alicia: My Story" so that their parents would also know the story. I am grateful to the parents who arranged for their children and other family members to share this knowledge.

I am honored to introduce a beautiful and wonderful teacher, Linda Goytia. She taught "Alicia: My Story" in her history and English classes. I was her guest speaker for twelve years. She prepared her students for my appearance in the manner of a true Holocaust scholar. The questions they asked were brilliant, seasoned with intelligence and compassion. They were very fortunate to have such a wonderful teacher and I am blessed to continue to have her as my very dear friend. I love you dearly, Linda.

Thank you my dear readers and friends who travel long distances to visit with me and ask questions. It is your love that kept me going when medically challenged. God bless you all.

Also from Desaware Publishing...

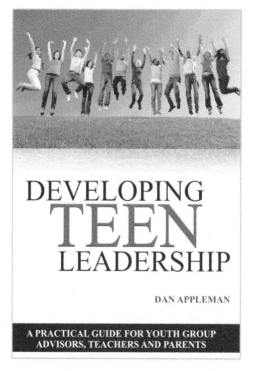

DEVELOPING
TEEN
LEADERSHIP

DAN APPLEMAN

A PRACTICAL GUIDE FOR YOUTH GROUP
ADVISORS, TEACHERS AND PARENTS

Not long ago, all it took to have a comfortable career was to do well in high school, get a college degree, and find a nice stable job. But today, good grades are not enough.

But there remain endless opportunities for those with real leadership skills - regardless of career choice.

Developing Teen Leadership covers virtually every topic today's parents, teachers and youth advisors need to help teens gain the leadership skills they will need in today's rapidly changing world.

www.teenleadershipbook.com

Notes

Made in the USA
Coppell, TX
07 October 2021

63519719R00056